Nashoba's "I SEE" Workbook

Language Expansion for Autism

Third Edition

Terresa York, MNM

Original artwork: Chad Jones

Graphic design: Jason Moore

Printed in the United States of America

10 9 8 7 6 5 4

First Edition Printing 2006, ©2006, Terresa York ISBN 978-1-4303-0577-4

Second Edition Printing 2010, ©2009, Terresa York ISBN 978-0-9826035-0-5

Third Edition Printing 2016, ©2016, Terresa York ISBN 978-0-9826035-3-6

©2016 Terresa York (third edition)

NAKIA E

ISBN 978-0-9826035-3-6

http://www.nashobasworkbooks.com

PREFACE

Prerequisite Skills

As a prerequisite, it is assumed that the child has basic reading skills and can write simple answers when prompted (or has use of a scribe).

How to use Nashoba's "I SEE" workbook

This workbook was designed to gradually increase a child's ability to describe what he or she sees by first isolating and then building upon individual attributes such as size, color, and shape. By breaking down the environment into a series of three-dimensional pictures, the child can begin to form descriptive language in a clear, concrete way through practice and repetition.

As a language expansion workbook, it is assumed that the child has already learned how to recognize colors, shapes, and other simple attributes and can write simple answers or sentences when prompted.

The lessons are intended to follow a logical order and should be taught as they are presented. In addition, each lesson builds upon itself resulting in an oral quiz. For that reason, it is best to complete the entire lesson in a single session, so that the information is retained as intended. However, if a lesson is interrupted, then a quick review of the previous material is recommended.

Finally, the goal is not to complete the work but to learn the skill. Lessons can and should be repeated as many times as necessary; pictures from home, school, magazines and books can be used to expand the lessons and to provide increased practice and repetition. The activities listed at the end of the workbook are intended to help the child generalize the emerging skills into other settings.

Other Helpful Hints

You may want to photo copy the lessons as you go along in case the child has trouble with any particular attribute. In that case, it would be good to repeat that attribute as many times as necessary before moving on.

In order to keep data on the oral quizzes, the teacher may want to write down what the child says under each question. In addition, a data collection table has been added at the end of the workbook in order to assist teachers and tutors in collecting data, sharing information, and recording observations.

CONTENTS

PART ONE

The attribute: COLOR (tell the color)

When we look at something, we see a picture of it with our eyes. It is easy to tell someone what we're looking at once we know how to describe the different parts of the picture.

The different parts of a picture are called attributes. Some attributes we will look at are color, size, shape, and texture.

We will also learn how to describe where someone or something is, what someone or something is doing, and what someone or something has possession of.

Using these skills, you will be able to answer the questions, "What are you looking at?" and "What do you see?"

Let's take these attributes one at a time.

1. Tell the color.

What color is this box?   _____

What color is this box?   _____

What color is this box?   _____

What color is this box?   _____

What color is this box?   _____

What color is this box?   _____

2. Now you are ready to answer the question, "What do you see?"
Continue to tell the color.

What do you see?   I see a white box.

What do you see?   _____

What do you see?   _____

What do you see?   _____

What do you see?   _____

What do you see?   _____

3. You are also ready to answer the question, "What are you looking at?" Continue to tell the color.

What are you looking at?   I'm looking at a white box.

What are you looking at?   _____

What are you looking at?   _____

What are you looking at?   _____

What are you looking at? 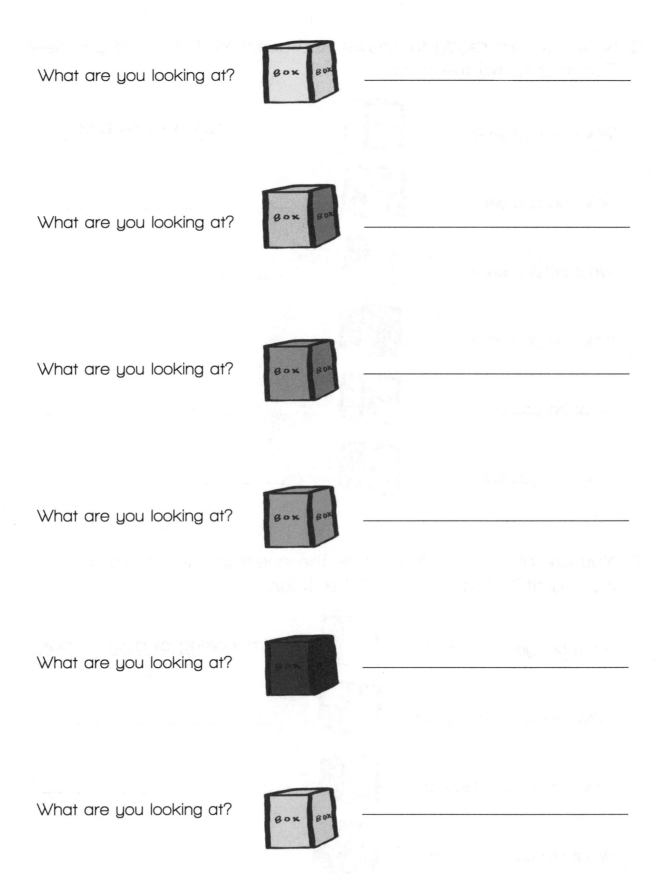 _____

What are you looking at? _____

What are you looking at? _____

What are you looking at? _____

What are you looking at? _____

What are you looking at? _____

4. Let's practice with some real pictures. Tell the color.

What do you see?   A ___blue___ ___bird___
                      (color)   (object)

What do you see?   A _____ _____
                      (color)   (object)

What do you see?   A _____ ___horse___
                      (color)   (object)

What do you see?
     A lady with a _____ ___dress___
                      (color)   (object)

What do you see?
     A ___and___ _____
       (two colors)   (object)

What do you see?   A _____ _____
                      (color)   (object)

What are you looking at?   A _____ _____
                                                     (color)   (object)

What are you looking at?   A _____ _____
                                                     (color)   (object)

What are you looking at?

      A _____ **and** _____ _____ **hat** _____
              (two colors)   (object)

Did you notice that sometimes you see more than one thing? When this happens you can focus on (or choose) just one thing to look at.

For example

What are you looking at? A **blue** **heart**.

In this picture, we see two doves, a heart, flowers, and stems. We were looking at the blue heart, but we could have also answered, *"A green stem, a white dove, or a purple flower."*

5. In the next pictures, let's choose just ONE thing to see or look at and answer the questions. Continue to tell the color.

What are you looking at? A <u>   </u> <u>**bow**</u>
                                      (color)   (object)

What are you looking at? A <u>   </u> <u>   </u>
                                      (color)   (object)

What are you looking at? A <u>   </u> <u>   </u>
                                      (color)   (object)

Did you also notice that sometimes the same thing can have more than one obvious color, so you have to name both colors?

For example   This penguin is clearly **black AND white**.

What are you looking at? A <u>**black and white**</u> <u>**penguin**</u>.

This party hat is clearly **blue AND yellow**.

What are you looking at? A <u>**blue and yellow**</u> <u>**hat**</u>.

6. Let's continue to tell the color in our answers. However, this time we will answer the question, "What do you see?"

What do you see? A ____blue____ ____bird____
(color)   (object)

What do you see? A _____ _____
(color)   (object)

What do you see? A _____ _____
(color)   (object)

What do you see?
    A lady with a _____ _____
(color)   (object)

What do you see?
    A ____and____ _____
(two colors)   (object)

What do you see? A _____ _____
(color)   (object)

What do you see?   A _____ _____
                        (color)   (object)

What do you see?   A _____ _____
                        (color)   (object)

What do you see?   A ____**and**____ _____
                        (color)   (object)

What do you see?   A _____ _____
                        (color)   (object)

What do you see?   A _____ _____
                        (color)   (object)

What do you see?   A _____ _____
                        (color)   (object)

15

Oral Quiz: Attribute "color"

Go get a friend or a teacher to ask you each question out loud, one at a time. Answer each question by telling the color and the object.

Example

What do you see?

What are you looking at?

(The teacher asks, "What do you see?" You answer, "I see a blue bird." The teacher asks, "What are you looking at?" You answer, "I'm looking at a blue bird.")

What do you see?

What are you looking at?

What do you see?

What are you looking at?

What do you see?

What are you looking at?

What do you see?

What are you looking at?

What do you see?　　What are you looking at?

What do you see?　　What are you looking at?

What do you see?　　What are you looking at?

What do you see?　　What are you looking at?

What do you see?　　What are you looking at?

What do you see?　　What are you looking at?

What do you see?　　What are you looking at?

PART TWO

The attribute: SIZE (tell the size)

Objects can be small, medium, large, big, little, tiny, huge, tall, wide, long, etc.

1. Size is easy, too.

What size is this box? (Circle)   Small   Medium   Large

What size is this box? (Circle)   Small   Medium   Large

What size is this box?  (Circle)   Small   Medium   Large

---

What size is this box?  (Circle)   Big   Little   Medium

What size is this box? (Circle)   Big   Little   Medium

What size is this box? (Circle)   Big   Little   Medium

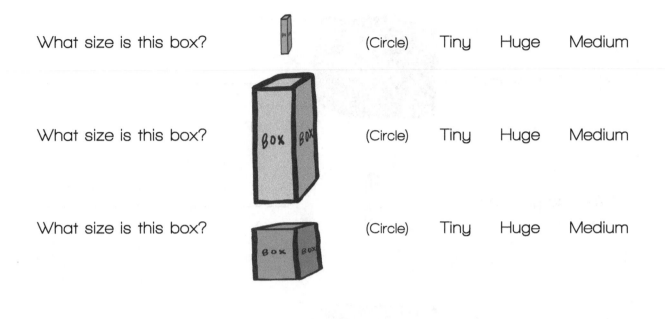

What size is this box?		(Circle)	Tiny	Huge	Medium
What size is this box?		(Circle)	Tiny	Huge	Medium
What size is this box?		(Circle)	Tiny	Huge	Medium

2. Now, you are ready to answer the question, "What do you see?" Tell the size.

Pick from

| Small | **Medium** | Large | **Tall** | Wide | **Long** |

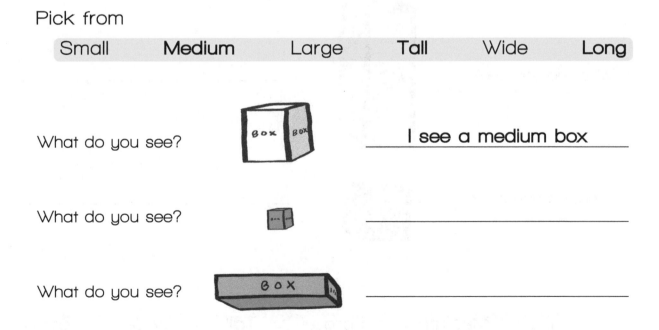

What do you see?   I see a medium box

What do you see?   _____

What do you see?   _____

What do you see? 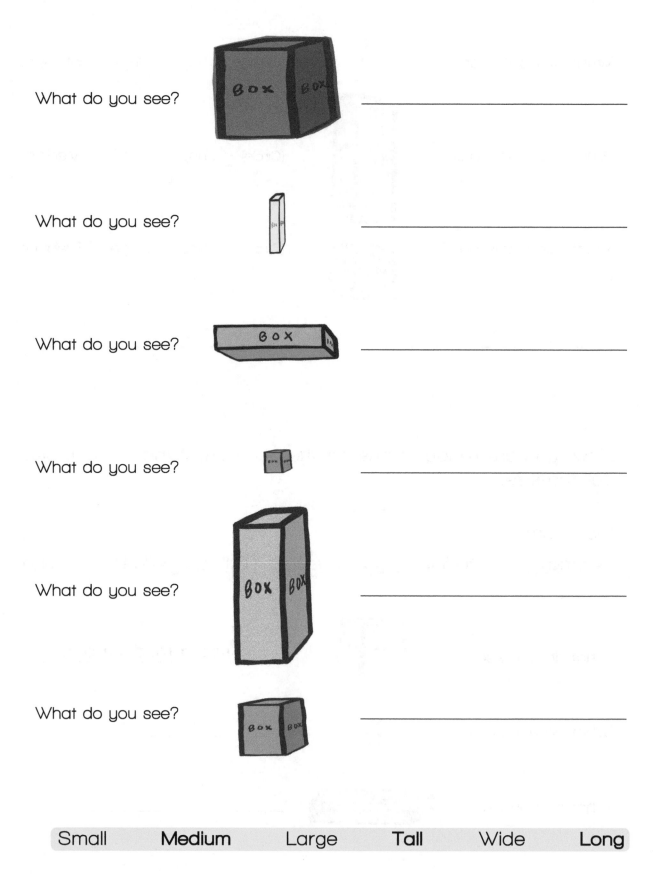 _____

What do you see? _____

What do you see? _____

What do you see? _____

What do you see? _____

What do you see? _____

| Small | **Medium** | Large | **Tall** | Wide | **Long** |

3. You are also ready to answer the question, "What are you looking at?" Tell the size.

Small	**Medium**	Large	**Tall**	Wide	**Long**

What are you looking at?   I'm looking at a medium box

What are you looking at?   _____

What are you looking at?   _____

What are you looking at?   _____

What are you looking at?   _____

What are you looking at?   _____

What are you looking at?  _____

What are you looking at? _____

What are you looking at?

_____

22

4. Look at the pictures below. Do you see that the size of each *picture* is about the same? However, some things are always considered to be large or small, wide or tall, just because of what they are. For example, giraffes are usually considered tall, while babies are usually considered small because they are such tiny people. A rhinoceros or an elephant would be considered a huge animal by anyone's standards, and ladybugs are very small insects.

Keeping this in mind, tell the size of the objects below.

Small	**Medium**	Large	**Tall**	Wide	**Long**

What are you looking at?   A _____   <u>ladybug</u>
                                    (size)   (object)

What are you looking at?   A _____   <u>elephant</u>
                                    (size)   (object)

What are you looking at?   A _____   <u>baby</u>
                                    (size)   (object)

What are you looking at?   A _____   _____
                                    (size)   (object)

5. You are now ready to answer the question, "What do you see?"
   Tell the size.

What do you see?   A _____ ladybug
                      (size)   (object)

What do you see?   A _____ _____
                      (size)   (object)

What do you see?   A _____ _____
                      (size)   (object)

What do you see?   A _____ _____
                      (size)   (object)

Oral Quiz: Attribute "size"

Go get a friend or a teacher to ask you each question out loud, one at a time. Answer each question by telling the size and the object.

Example

What do you see?   What are you looking at?

(The teacher asks, "What do you see?" You answer, "I see a small baby." The teacher asks, "What are you looking at?" You answer, "I'm looking at a small baby.")

What do you see?   What are you looking at?

What do you see?   What are you looking at?

What do you see?   What are you looking at?

What do you see?  What are you looking at?

What do you see?  What are you looking at?

What do you see?  What are you looking at?

What do you see?  What are you looking at?

PART THREE

The attributes SIZE and COLOR together

Let's put size and color together. Fill in the blanks then write it in a sentence.

1. Example

What are you looking at?   A <u>small</u> <u>blue</u> <u>bird</u>
                                (size)   (color) (object)

I am looking at a small blue bird.

2. What are you looking at?

A _____ _____ _____
   (size)   (color)   (object)

I am

3. What are you looking at?

A <u>tall</u> _____ _____
   (size)   (color)   (object)

I am

4. What are you looking at?

A _____ _____ _____
    (size)   (color)   (object)

I am _____

5. What are you looking at?

A _____ _____ _____
    (size)   (color)   (object)

I am _____

6. What are you looking at?

A _____ _____ _____
    (size)   (color)   (object)

I am _____

7. What are you looking at?

A _____ _____ _____
    (size)   (color)   (object)

I am _____

8. What are you looking at?

A _____ _____ _____
    (size)   (color)   (object)

I am _____

9. What are you looking at?

A _____ _____ **dog**
    (size)   (color)   (object)

I am _____

10. What are you looking at?

A _____ _____ _____
     (size)   (color)   (object)

I am _____

11. What are you looking at?

A _____ **red and** _____
     (size)   (color)   (object)

A _____ _____ **leaf**
     (size)   (color)   (object)

I am _____

I am _____

PART FOUR

The attribute: SHAPE (tell the shape)

1. Tell the shape.

What shape is this?   This is a _____

What shape is this?   _____

What shape is this?   _____

What shape is this?   This is a moon _____

2. Now, you are ready to answer the question, "What do you see?"
   Tell the shape.

What shape is this?   I see a _____

What shape is this?   _____

What shape is this?   _____

What shape is this?   _____

3. You are also ready to answer the question, "What are you looking at?"

Tell the shape.

What are you looking at?

I am looking at a _____

What are you looking at?

_____

What are you looking at?

I am looking at a _____

What are you looking at?

_____

4. Let's practice on some real pictures. Tell the shape.

Pick from

circle   square   moon   triangle

Example

What do you see?

I see a watch shaped like a _____.

What do you see?

I see a _____ shaped like a _____.

What do you see?

_____ shaped like a _____.

What do you see?

_____.

5. Let's answer the question, "What are you looking at?"
Tell the shape.

What are you looking at?

I'm looking at a watch shaped like a _____.

What are you looking at?

I'm looking at a _____ shaped like a _____.

What are you looking at?

I'm looking at _____.

What are you looking at?

_____.

34

Oral Quiz: Attribute "shape"

Go get a friend or a teacher to ask you each question out loud, one at a time. Answer each question by telling the shape and the object.

What do you see?  What are you looking at?

What do you see?  What are you looking at?

What do you see?  What are you looking at?

What do you see?  What are you looking at?

What do you see?  What are you looking at?

What do you see?  What are you looking at?

PART FIVE

The attribute: TEXTURE (tell the texture)

Texture describes how something feels when you touch it. Things you touch can be soft or hard, bumpy or smooth, or even prickly or rough. Answer the following questions by telling the object's texture.

Pick from

| soft | hard | wet | prickly |

1. "What do you see?" Tell the texture.

What do you see?   I see a soft kitten. _____

What do you see?   I see a hard _____

What do you see?   _____

What do you see?   _____

What do you see?   _____

1. Answer the question, "what you are looking at?" Tell the texture.

Pick from

| soft | hard | wet | prickly |

What are you looking at?   _____

                                         _____

What are you looking at?   _____

                                         _____

What are you looking at?   _____

                                         _____

What are you looking at?   _____

                                         _____

What are you looking at?   _____

                                         _____

Go get a friend or a teacher to ask you each question out loud, one at a time. Answer each question by telling the texture and the object.

| soft | hard | wet | prickly |

What do you see?   What are you looking at?

What do you see?   What are you looking at?

What do you see?   What are you looking at?

What do you see?   What are you looking at?

What do you see?   What are you looking at?

PART SIX

Combining Shape and Texture

Let's put shape and texture together. Fill in the blanks then write it in a sentence.

Example

What are you looking at?   A ___soft___ ___square___ ___dog___
                              (texture)   (shape)   (object)

I am looking at a soft, square dog. _____

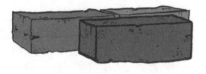

1. What do you see?

A _____ _____ ___brick___
  (texture)   (shape)   (object)

I see _____

2. What are you looking at?

A _____ ___round___ _____
  (texture)   (shape)   (object)

I am _____

3. What do you see?

A _____ **triangular** _____
    (texture)   (shape)   (object)

I see a _____

4. What are you looking at?

A _____ _____ _____
    (texture)   (shape)   (object)

I am _____

5. What do you see?

A _____ **round** _____
    (texture)   (shape)   (object)

I see a _____

PART SEVEN

The attribute: WHERE SOMETHING IS (tell where something is)

Things can be in, on, under, beside, below, behind, above, in front of, or next to other things.

Example

Where is the fruit? __On the table__

What are you looking at? __I am looking at fruit on a table.__

What do you see? __I see__

1. Where is the boy? _____

   What are you looking at? _____

   What do you see? _____

2. Where is the bow? _____

   What are you looking at? _____

   What do you see? _____

3. Where is the pumpkin? _____

   What are you looking at? _____

   What do you see? _____

4. Where is the box? <u>Beneath the</u> _____

   What are you looking at? _____

   What do you see? _____

5. Where is the mop? _____

   What are you looking at? _____

   What do you see? _____

   Where is the bucket? _____

   What are you looking at? _____

   What do you see? _____

6. Where is the green balloon? _____

   What are you looking at? _____

   What do you see? _____

   Where is the red balloon? _____

   What are you looking at? _____

   What do you see? _____

7. Where is the boy? _____

What are you looking at? _____

What do you see? _____

Where is the bike? _____

What are you looking at? _____

What do you see? _____

8. Where is the butterfly? _____

What are you looking at? _____

What do you see? _____

Where is the leaf? _____

What are you looking at? _____

What do you see? _____

9. Where is the cat? _____

What are you looking at? _____

What do you see? _____

Where is the moon?_____

What are you looking at? _____

What do you see? _____

10. Where is the bow? _____

What are you looking at? _____

What do you see? _____

Where is the card? _____

What are you looking at? _____

What do you see? _____

Go get a friend or a teacher to ask you each question out loud, one at a time. Answer each question by telling where the object or person is in relation to something else.

Example

What are you looking at?

I'm looking at a boy in a bed.

What do you see?

I see a boy in a bed.

What are you looking at?

What do you see?

What are you looking at?

What do you see?

What are you looking at?

What do you see?

What are you looking at?

What do you see?

PART EIGHT

The attribute: WHAT SOMEONE OR SOMETHING IS DOING
(tell what the object or subject is doing)

People and animals can be doing all kinds of things. They can eat, run, play and sleep, just to name a few. Even objects can be doing something. For example, the sun can be shining, and the snow can be falling.

Look at each picture and tell what the character is doing. Then answer the questions, "What do you see?" and "What are you looking at?"

Example

What is the black horse doing?

　　　The black horse is jumping over the fence.

What do you see?

　　　I see a black horse jumping over a fence.

What are you looking at?

　　　I am looking at a black horse jumping over a fence.

What is the man doing?　__The man is riding a horse.__

What do you see?　_____

What are you looking at?　__I am looking at__ _____

What are the men doing?　__The men are playing hockey.__

What do you see?　_____

What are you looking at?　_____

46

What are the kids doing? _____

What do you see? _____

What are you looking at? _____

What is this couple doing? _____

What do you see? _____

What are you looking at? _____

What is the boy doing? _____

What do you see? _____

What are you looking at? _____

What is this couple doing? __They are_____

What do you see? _____

What are you looking at? _____

What is the woman doing? _____

What do you see? _____

What are you looking at? _____

What is the man doing? _____

What do you see? _____

What are you looking at? _____

What is this boy doing? _____

What do you see? _____

What are you looking at? _____

What is this girl doing? _____

What do you see? _____

What are you looking at? _____

Oral Quiz: Attribute "what someone or something is doing"

Go get a friend or a teacher to ask you each question out loud, one at a time. Answer each question by telling what the object or subject is doing.

Example

What do you see?

I see a man riding a horse.

What are you looking at?

I'm looking at a man riding a horse.

What do you see?

What are you looking at?

What do you see?

What are you looking at?

What do you see?

What are you looking at?

What do you see?

What are you looking at?

What do you see?

What are you looking at?

What do you see?

What are you looking at?

What do you see?

What are you looking at?

What do you see?

What are you looking at?

PART NINE

The attribute: WHAT SOMEONE OR SOMETHING HAS POSSESSION OF
(tell what the object or subject has)

People and animals can have all kinds of things. A football player can have a football, a woman can have a hat, a child can have an ice cream cone, etc.

Look at each picture and tell what the character HAS. Then answer the questions, "What do you see?" and "What are you looking at?"

Example

What does this bear have?
> **The bear has a red heart.**

What do you see?
> **I see a bear with a red heart.**

What are you looking at?
> **I'm looking at a bear with a red heart.**

What does this dog have? **The dog has a bone.**

What do you see? _____

What are you looking at? _____

What does this cat have? **The cat has a** _____

What do you see? _____

What are you looking at? _____

What does this little girl have? _____

What do you see? _____

What are you looking at? _____

What does this monkey have? _____

What do you see? _____

What are you looking at? _____

What does this cat have? _____

What do you see? _____

What are you looking at? _____

What does this pirate have? **The pirate has** _____

What do you see? _____

What are you looking at? _____

What does this couple have? _____

What do you see? _____

What are you looking at? _____

What does this man have? _____

What do you see? _____

What are you looking at? _____

What does this baby have? _____

What do you see? _____

What are you looking at? _____

Go get a friend or a teacher to ask you each question out loud, one at a time. Answer each question by telling what the object or subject HAS.

Example

What do you see?

I see a bear with a heart.

What are you looking at?

I'm looking at a bear with a heart.

What do you see?

What are you looking at?

What do you see?

What are you looking at?

What do you see?

What are you looking at?

What do you see?

What are you looking at?

What do you see?

What are you looking at?

What do you see?

What are you looking at?

What do you see?

What are you looking at?

What do you see?

What are you looking at?

Putting it all together

Whenever you look at something, you are seeing a picture with your eyes. As you have learned, that picture may have a size, shape, color, or texture. The object or character you are looking at is always someplace specific, and may be *doing something or have possession of something*. With all of these attributes to choose from, it is easy to describe what you see to someone else. You simply choose one thing at a time and describe its attributes.

On the following pages, you will be shown several detailed pictures. There will be a box at the top of each page listing all of the attributes you have learned in this workbook. Answer the questions, "what do you see" and "what are you looking at" by describing the attributes one at a time. Some pictures may have all seven of the attributes you learned, while others may only have three or four. Use as many attributes as you can for each picture.

Example   "What do you see?"

a. Color

b. Size (Big, small, medium, tall, wide, long, etc.)

c. Shape (round, square, triangular, etc.)

d. Texture (soft, hard, wet, prickly, etc.)

e. WHERE someone or something is

f. What someone or something IS DOING

g. What someone or something HAS

a. color — I see a cat with a pink bow.

b. size — I see a small cat.

c. shape — I see two round eyes.

d. texture — I see a soft, furry cat.

e. where it is — I see a cat next to a pair of scissors.

f. what it is doing — I see a cat getting its hair done.

g. what it has — I see a cat with a comb, mirror, and scissors.

a. Color

b. Size

c. Shape

d. Texture

e. WHERE someone or something is

f. What someone or something IS DOING

g. What someone or something HAS

What are you looking at?

a. _____

_____

b. _____

_____

c. _____

_____

d. _____

_____

e. _____

_____

f. _____

_____

g. _____

_____

a. Color

b. Size

c. Shape

d. Texture

e. WHERE someone or something is

f. What someone or something IS DOING

g. What someone or something HAS

What do you see?

a. _____

_____

b. _____

_____

c. _____

_____

d. _____

_____

e. _____

_____

f. _____

_____

g. _____

_____

a. Color

b. Size

c. Shape

d. Texture

e. WHERE someone or something is

f. What someone or something IS DOING

g. What someone or something HAS

What are you looking at?

a. _____

_____

b. _____

_____

c. _____

_____

d. _____

_____

e. _____

_____

f. _____

_____

g. _____

_____

a. Color

b. Size

c. Shape

d. Texture

e. WHERE someone or something is

f. What someone or something IS DOING

g. What someone or something HAS

What do you see?

a. _____

_____

b. _____

_____

c. _____

_____

d. _____

_____

e. _____

_____

f. _____

_____

g. _____

_____

a. Color

b. Size

c. Shape

d. Texture

e. WHERE someone or something is

f. What someone or something IS DOING

g. What someone or something HAS

What are you looking at?

a. _____

_____

b. _____

_____

c. _____

_____

d. _____

_____

e. _____

_____

f. _____

_____

g. _____

_____

Now you try answering the questions without any hints. Write a sentence about one thing you see in each picture using at least three attributes.

What are you looking at?

_____

_____

_____

_____

What do you see?

_____

_____

_____

_____

What are you looking at?

_____

_____

_____

_____

What do you see?

_____

_____

_____

_____

What are you looking at?

_____

_____

_____

_____

What do you see?

_____

_____

_____

_____

What are you looking at?

_____

_____

_____

_____

What do you see?

_____

_____

_____

_____

What are you looking at?

_____

_____

_____

_____

What do you see?

_____

_____

_____

_____

Activity One

Go on a walk with your teacher. Your teacher will point to things and ask you, "What do you see?" Answer the question using as many attributes as you can.

Activity Two

Get out a bunch of toys with your teacher or a friend. Take turns holding up each toy and asking the question, "What are you looking at?" Answer the question using as many attributes as you can.

Activity Three

Find a picture book. Look at the pictures and write down answers to both questions on a separate sheet of paper. What are you looking at? I am looking at... What do you see? I see...

Activity Four

Try to remember someplace you have gone in the past — maybe on a vacation, to a swimming pool, or on a hike in the mountains. If you want, you can draw a picture of it. It also helps to close your eyes and imagine the place. Now, describe what you see (what you are remembering) to your teacher or a friend using as many attributes as you can.

Cut out or copy this chart for use in other settings.

Attribute Chart

Attributes

1. Color: Red, blue, green, orange, yellow, pink, purple, white, etc.

2. Size: Big, small, short, tall, wide, skinny, medium, long etc.

3. Shape: Circular, square-shaped, moon-shaped, triangular, etc.

4. Texture: Soft, hard, smooth, wet, prickly, etc.

5. Where someone or something is: In, on, under, beside, below, above, behind, in front of, next to, etc.

6. What someone or something is doing: Talking, laughing, playing, jumping, singing, etc.

7. What someone or something has possession of: The dog has a bone, the man has a wallet, the woman has a purse, etc.

Data Collection & Notes

Date _____   Lesson # <u>One</u> _____

                                        Page(s) _____

% of accuracy _____   Suggestions: Repeat Lesson

# of prompts _____   Review Lesson

                                                      Other _____

Observations

_____

_____

_____

_____

Other

_____

_____

_____

_____

Name or Initials of teacher/tutor _____

- -

Date _____   Lesson # <u>Two</u> _____

                                        Page(s) _____

% of accuracy _____   Suggestions: Repeat Lesson

# of prompts _____   Review Lesson

                                                      Other _____

Observations

_____

_____

_____

_____

Other

_____

_____

_____

_____

Name or Initials of teacher/tutor _____

Date _____   Lesson # <u>Three</u>_____
                                   Page(s) _____

% of accuracy _____   Suggestions: Repeat Lesson
# of prompts _____   Review Lesson
                                             Other _____

Observations

_____

_____

_____

_____

Other

_____

_____

_____

_____

Name or Initials of teacher/tutor _____

- -

Date _____   Lesson # <u>Four</u>_____
                                   Page(s) _____

% of accuracy _____   Suggestions: Repeat Lesson
# of prompts _____   Review Lesson
                                             Other _____

Observations

_____

_____

_____

_____

Other

_____

_____

_____

_____

Name or Initials of teacher/tutor _____

Date _____ Lesson # **Five** _____

                                        Page(s) _____

% of accuracy _____ Suggestions: Repeat Lesson
# of prompts _____   Review Lesson
                                                     Other _____

Observations

_____
_____
_____
_____

Other

_____
_____
_____
_____

Name or Initials of teacher/tutor _____

- -

Date _____ Lesson # **Six** _____

                                         Page(s) _____

% of accuracy _____ Suggestions: Repeat Lesson
# of prompts _____   Review Lesson
                                                     Other _____

Observations

_____
_____
_____
_____

Other

_____
_____
_____
_____

Name or Initials of teacher/tutor _____

Date _____   Lesson # __Seven_____
                                    Page(s)   _____

% of accuracy _____   Suggestions: Repeat Lesson
# of prompts   _____   Review Lesson
                                                   Other _____

Observations

_____
_____
_____
_____

Other

_____
_____
_____
_____

Name or Initials of teacher/tutor _____

- -

Date _____   Lesson # __Eight_____
                                    Page(s)   _____

% of accuracy _____   Suggestions: Repeat Lesson
# of prompts   _____   Review Lesson
                                                   Other _____

Observations

_____
_____
_____
_____

Other

_____
_____
_____
_____

Name or Initials of teacher/tutor _____

Date _____ Lesson # **Nine** _____
                                 Page(s) _____

% of accuracy _____ Suggestions: Repeat Lesson
# of prompts _____   Review Lesson
                                         Other _____

Observations

_____

_____

_____

_____

Other

_____

_____

_____

_____

Name or Initials of teacher/tutor _____

- -

Date _____ Lesson # **Putting it together**
                                 Page(s) _____

% of accuracy _____ Suggestions: Repeat Lesson
# of prompts _____   Review Lesson
                                         Other _____

Observations

_____

_____

_____

_____

Other

_____

_____

_____

_____

Name or Initials of teacher/tutor _____

Date _____   Lesson #   <u>Practice Activities</u>

                                           Page(s) _____

% of accuracy _____   Suggestions: Repeat Lesson
# of prompts _____   Review Lesson
                                           Other _____

Observations

_____

_____

_____

_____

Other

_____

_____

_____

_____

Name or Initials of teacher/tutor _____

- -

Date _____   Lesson # _____

                                           Page(s) _____

% of accuracy _____   Suggestions: Repeat Lesson
# of prompts _____   Review Lesson
                                           Other _____

Observations

_____

_____

_____

_____

Other

_____

_____

_____

_____

Name or Initials of teacher/tutor _____

OTHER AVAILABLE WORKBOOKS AND MATERIALS

The *Nashoba's Learning System* includes a series of Language Expansion, Math Curriculum, and Reading Comprehension Workbooks designed to provide educators and parents with readily available tools to help teach children on the Autism Spectrum or children with visual, concrete learning styles.

The hands-on series was designed to be used without the need for further lesson planning or a formal teaching background and to travel easily with the child between learning environments.

For further information and to see new releases, please visit:
http://www.nashobasworkbooks.com